50 | PROVEN WAYS TO MARKET YOUR LIFE COACHING BUSINESS

YOUR ULTIMATE GUIDE TO GETTING CLIENTS + GROWING YOUR BUSINESS

JOEEL A. RIVERA, M.ED. + NATALIE RIVERA

50 PROVEN WAYS TO MARKET YOUR LIFE COACHING BUSINESS

by Joeel A. Rivera M.Ed. and Natalie Rivera

Copyright © 2024 Transformation Publishing

 **TRANSFORMATION** PUBLISHING

ISBN: 9798328224932

SPECIAL OFFER: receive 50% off top-rated business courses and life coach certifications through Transformation Academy. See the final page for details or visit: TransformationAcademy.com/50ways

| WELCOME

Welcome to **"50 Proven Ways to Market Your Life Coaching Business"** – your ultimate guide to supercharging your coaching practice! Whether you're a seasoned coach or just starting out, this mini book is packed with actionable strategies designed to help you attract new clients, build your brand, and grow your business.

WHY THIS MINI BOOK?

Let's face it: running a coaching business can feel like juggling flaming swords while riding a unicycle. But don't worry, we're here to make sure you don't get burned. This mini book is your safety net, offering you a treasure trove of marketing tools that will help you thrive in today's competitive landscape. Here's what you'll get out of this book:

> ➤ **Diverse Strategies**: From social media to public speaking, we've covered all the bases. No stone is left unturned, and no marketing opportunity is left unexplored.

> ➤ **Practical Steps**: Each strategy comes with a step-by-step guide, best practices, real-life examples, and an action plan to ensure you can hit the ground running.

> ➤ **Flexibility**: Whether you prefer the digital world or face-to-face interactions, there's something here for everyone.

> ➢ **Consistency Tips**: Learn the importance of staying consistent in your efforts, because success doesn't come overnight – it comes to those who persist.

> ➢ **Adaptability**: Discover the value of tweaking and adapting strategies to fit your unique style and the needs of your clients.

Choosing Your Strategies

Think of this mini book as a buffet – you don't have to (and shouldn't) eat everything at once. Pick the strategies that resonate most with you and your business. Are you a social butterfly? Dive into networking events and social media. Prefer creating valuable content? Focus on blogs, podcasts, or webinars. Here's how to make the most of it:

> ➢ **Assess Your Strengths**: Choose strategies that play to your strengths. If you're a great speaker, look at public speaking or webinars. If you love writing, dive into content creation.

> ➢ **Know Your Audience**: Consider where your potential clients spend their time. Are they on LinkedIn, attending local events, or reading industry publications?

> ➢ **Set Clear Goals**: Define what you want to achieve. More clients? Greater visibility? Stronger community engagement? Your goals will guide your strategy choices.

> ➢ **Start Small**: Don't overwhelm yourself by trying to implement everything at once. Pick a few strategies, execute them well, and then expand.

The Importance of Consistency

Consistency is the secret sauce in any successful marketing plan. It's like brushing your teeth – you can't do it once and expect perfect teeth forever (unless you're a superhero with invincible enamel). Similarly, you need to consistently apply your marketing strategies to see results. Whether it's posting regularly on social media, attending networking events monthly, or sending out newsletters, keep at it.

EMBRACE THE LEARNING CURVE

Here's the reality check: not all strategies will work on your first try. Just like you didn't master riding a bike without a few scrapes, you won't master these strategies without some trial and error. But that's okay! Marketing is an evolving practice, and what works for one coach might need tweaking for another.

Remember, Edison didn't invent the light bulb on his first attempt – he had 1,000 unsuccessful tries. So if your first webinar doesn't attract a crowd or your first ad campaign falls flat, don't despair. Adapt, tweak, and try again. Each attempt gets you closer to finding what works best for you and the people you serve.

A DASH OF HUMOR

If all else fails, remember to keep your sense of humor. Marketing can be as unpredictable as trying to teach a cat to fetch. But with persistence, creativity, and a willingness to learn, you'll find your groove. And who knows? You might even enjoy the journey!

So, get ready to dive in, experiment, and most importantly, have fun! The world of marketing is full of opportunities, and with the right tools, you're well on your way to becoming a marketing maestro for your coaching business. Let's get started!

TABLE OF CONTENTS

CHAPTER 1:
NETWORKING AND CLIENT ENGAGEMENT

1. ATTEND NETWORKING EVENTS

Introduction:

➤ Networking events provide opportunities to meet potential clients and industry peers.

➤ Building relationships at these events can lead to referrals and new business opportunities.

Step-by-Step Guide:

➤ **Research Events**: Find relevant events in your area or online.

➤ **Prepare Your Pitch**: Have a concise introduction ready about who you are and what you do.

➤ **Bring Business Cards**: Ensure you have enough business cards to hand out.

➤ **Engage in Conversations**: Be genuine and interested in others 'stories and needs.

➤ **Follow Up**: Connect with people you met within 24-48 hours after the event.

Best Practices:

- ➢ **Active Listening**: Show genuine interest in what others are saying.
- ➢ **Value Offering**: Offer advice or help where possible, rather than just selling your services.

Real-Life Examples:

- ➢ **Case Study**: Sarah attended a local business networking event and secured two new clients by following up with personalized emails.

Measurement and Evaluation:

- ➢ **Connections Made**: Count the number of meaningful connections.
- ➢ **Leads Generated**: Track the number of leads and follow-ups.

Additional Resources:

- ➢ **Books:** "Networking Like a Pro" by Ivan Misner.
- ➢ **Online Courses:** Life Coach Business Masterclass TransformationAcademy.com/getclients

Action Plan:

- ➢ **Checklist:**
  - o Research and register for events.
  - o Prepare pitch and business cards.
  - o Engage and collect contacts.
  - o Follow up.
- ➢ **Timeline:**
  - o Week 1: Research and register.
  - o Week 2: Prepare pitch and materials.

- o Week 3: Attend event.
- o Week 4: Follow up with contacts.

2. JOIN PROFESSIONAL ASSOCIATIONS

Introduction:

➢ Professional associations offer credibility and networking opportunities.

➢ Membership can lead to collaborations, referrals, and access to resources.

Step-by-Step Guide:

➢ **Identify Associations**: Find relevant associations in your coaching niche.

➢ **Apply for Membership**: Follow the application process and pay any fees.

➢ **Participate Actively**: Attend meetings, join committees, and contribute to discussions.

➢ **Leverage Resources**: Utilize member resources like directories and forums.

Best Practices:

➢ **Active Participation**: Engage in association activities to build visibility.

➢ **Networking**: Use association events to network with peers.

Real-Life Examples:

➢ **Case Study**: John joined the International Coach Federation and gained valuable connections and clients through active participation.

Measurement and Evaluation:

- ➢ **Membership Benefits**: Track the resources and connections gained.
- ➢ **Client Referrals**: Measure the number of clients referred through the association.

Additional Resources:

- ➢ **Books**: "The Value of Membership" by Marjorie Hass.
- ➢ **Online Resources:** Life Coach Business Masterclass TransformationAcademy.com/getclients

Action Plan:

- ➢ **Checklist:**
  - o Research associations.
  - o Apply and pay membership fees.
  - o Participate in activities.
  - o Leverage resources.
- ➢ **Timeline:**
  - o Week 1: Identify and apply for membership.
  - o Week 2: Participate in introductory activities.
  - o Ongoing: Engage in association events and resources.

3. HOST FREE WORKSHOPS

Introduction:

- ➢ Free workshops are a great way to showcase your expertise and attract clients.
- ➢ They provide hands-on experience and demonstrate the value of your coaching.

Step-by-Step Guide:

➢ **Choose a Topic**: Select a relevant topic that addresses common client needs.

➢ **Plan Content**: Outline the workshop structure, key points, and takeaways.

➢ **Promote the Workshop**: Use social media, email marketing, and local ads.

➢ **Prepare Materials**: Create handouts, slides, and other resources.

➢ **Host the Workshop**: Engage participants with interactive elements.

➢ **Follow Up**: Send thank-you emails and additional resources, including a call-to-action.

Best Practices:

➢ **Interactive Elements**: Use Q&A sessions, group activities, and live demonstrations.

➢ **Clear Value Proposition**: Ensure participants understand the benefits they'll gain.

Real-Life Examples:

➢ **Case Study**: Jane hosted a workshop on time management and gained several new clients by following up with personalized offers.

Measurement and Evaluation:

➢ **Attendance Numbers**: Track the number of participants.

➢ **Engagement Levels**: Measure engagement through participation and feedback.

➢ **Conversion Rate**: Calculate the percentage of attendees who become clients.

Additional Resources:

➢ **Books**: "Workshop Planning and Presentation" by Michael Sloan.

➢ Online Courses: Life Coach Business Masterclass TransformationAcademy.com/getclients

Action Plan:

➢ **Checklist:**

  o Choose a topic.
  o Plan content.
  o Set date and time.
  o Promote workshop.
  o Prepare materials.
  o Host workshop.
  o Follow up.

➢ **Timeline:**

  o Week 1: Select topic and plan content.
  o Week 2: Promote workshop.
  o Week 3: Finalize preparations.
  o Week 4: Host and follow up.

4. OFFER COMPLIMENTARY COACHING SESSIONS

Introduction:

➢ Complimentary sessions give potential clients a firsthand experience of your coaching.

> They build trust and showcase your coaching style and effectiveness.

Step-by-Step Guide:

> **Define Your Offer**: Decide on the duration and format of the complimentary session.

> **Promote the Offer**: Use your website, social media, and email marketing to advertise.

> **Schedule Sessions**: Use a scheduling tool to manage bookings.

> **Conduct the Session**: Focus on providing value and addressing the client's needs.

> **Follow Up**: Send a thank-you email with a special offer for ongoing coaching.

Best Practices:

> **Personalized Approach**: Tailor the session to the individual's specific needs.

> **Clear Next Steps**: Provide clear recommendations and next steps for continued coaching.

Real-Life Examples:

> **Case Study**: Emily offered a free initial session and converted 30% of attendees into paying clients.

Measurement and Evaluation:

> **Number of Sessions**: Track how many complimentary sessions are conducted.

> **Conversion Rate**: Measure the percentage of sessions that convert to paying clients.

Additional Resources:

- ➢ **Books**: "The Art of Selling Coaching" by Nikki Owen.
- ➢ **Tools**: Scheduling tools like Calendly or Acuity.
- ➢ **Online Course:** Life Coach Business Masterclass TransformationAcademy.com/getclients

Action Plan:

- ➢ **Checklist:**
  - o Define offer.
  - o Promote offer.
  - o Schedule sessions.
  - o Conduct sessions.
  - o Follow up.
- ➢ **Timeline:**
  - o Week 1: Define and promote offer.
  - o Ongoing: Schedule and conduct sessions.
  - o Week 4: Follow up with participants.

5. ENGAGE IN SOCIAL MEDIA GROUPS

Introduction:

- ➢ Social media groups are a great platform to engage with potential clients and showcase your expertise.
- ➢ They offer opportunities for networking, sharing knowledge, and building relationships.

Step-by-Step Guide:

- ➢ **Identify Relevant Groups**: Find groups on Facebook, LinkedIn, and other platforms related to your niche.

➤ **Join and Introduce Yourself**: Join the group and introduce yourself and your expertise.

➤ **Provide Value**: Regularly share valuable content, answer questions, and engage in discussions.

➤ **Promote Discreetly**: Share your services and offers subtly, focusing on providing value first.

➤ **Build Relationships**: Connect with group members individually and offer free consultations.

Best Practices:

➤ **Consistency**: Engage regularly to build visibility and trust.

➤ **Value-First Approach**: Focus on providing value before promoting your services.

Real-Life Examples:

➤ **Case Study**: Mike engaged in a LinkedIn group for small business owners and gained several clients by consistently providing valuable advice.

Measurement and Evaluation:

➤ **Engagement Levels**: Track the number of posts, comments, and likes.

➤ **Leads Generated**: Measure the number of leads and follow-ups from group engagements.

Additional Resources:

➤ **Books**: "Social Media Marketing for Coaches" by Adam Hommey.

Action Plan:

> **Checklist:**
> - o Identify and join groups.
> - o Introduce yourself.
> - o Engage regularly.
> - o Promote discreetly.
> - o Build relationships.

> **Timeline:**
> - o Week 1: Join and introduce yourself.
> - o Ongoing: Engage and provide value.
> - o Week 4: Follow up with individual connections.

6. SPEAK AT LOCAL EVENTS

Introduction:

> Speaking at local events establishes you as an authority and connects you with potential clients.

> It provides a platform to share your expertise and offer valuable insights.

Step-by-Step Guide:

> **Identify Events**: Find local business, community, and industry events where you can speak.

> **Pitch Your Topic**: Propose a topic that is relevant and valuable to the audience.

> **Prepare Your Presentation**: Create an engaging and informative presentation.

> **Promote Your Appearance**: Use your network and social media to promote your speaking engagement.

➤ **Engage the Audience**: Deliver your presentation and engage with the audience through Q&A sessions.

➤ **Follow Up**: Connect with attendees and offer additional resources or consultations.

Best Practices:

➤ **Practice**: Rehearse your presentation to ensure smooth delivery.

➤ **Engagement**: Encourage audience interaction and questions.

Real-Life Examples:

➤ **Case Study**: Laura spoke at a local business expo and gained several new clients by offering free follow-up consultations.

Measurement and Evaluation:

➤ **Audience Size**: Track the number of attendees.

➤ **Engagement Levels**: Measure audience engagement through questions and feedback.

➤ **Leads Generated**: Track the number of leads and follow-ups from the event.

Additional Resources:

➤ **Books**: "Talk Like TED" by Carmine Gallo.

➤ **Online Courses**: Life Coach Business Masterclass TransformationAcademy.com/getclients

Action Plan:

➤ **Checklist:**
   o Identify events.
   o Pitch topic.

o   Prepare presentation.

o   Promote appearance.

o   Engage audience.

o   Follow up.

➢ **Timeline:**

o   Week 1: Identify and pitch events.

o   Week 2: Prepare presentation.

o   Week 3: Promote appearance.

o   Week 4: Deliver presentation and follow up.

7. LEVERAGE PERSONAL NETWORK

Introduction:

➢ Your personal network can be a valuable source of referrals and clients.

➢ Building and nurturing relationships within your network can lead to new business opportunities.

Step-by-Step Guide:

➢ **Identify Key Contacts**: List friends, family, and colleagues who might be able to refer clients.

➢ **Reach Out**: Send personalized messages or emails to let them know about your coaching services.

➢ **Offer Incentives**: Provide referral bonuses or discounts for referred clients.

➢ **Stay Connected**: Regularly update your network on your services and successes.

➢ **Show Appreciation**: Thank those who refer clients and keep them informed of the results.

Best Practices:

- ➤ **Personalized Communication**: Tailor your messages to each contact.
- ➤ **Consistent Follow-Up**: Keep your network engaged with regular updates.

Real-Life Examples:

- ➤ **Case Study**: Tom leveraged his personal network and gained five new clients by offering a referral discount.

Measurement and Evaluation:

- ➤ **Referrals Generated**: Track the number of referrals from your network.
- ➤ **Conversion Rate**: Measure the percentage of referrals that convert to clients.

Additional Resources:

- ➤ **Books**: "Endless Referrals" by Bob Burg.
- ➤ **Online Courses**: Life Coach Business Masterclass TransformationAcademy.com/getclients

Action Plan:

- ➤ **Checklist:**
  - o Identify key contacts.
  - o Reach out with personalized messages.
  - o Offer incentives.
  - o Stay connected.
  - o Show appreciation.
- ➤ **Timeline:**

- o Week 1: Identify and reach out to contacts.
- o Ongoing: Offer incentives and stay connected.
- o Week 4: Follow up and show appreciation.

8. FOLLOW UP WITH PAST CLIENTS

Introduction:

➤ Past clients can be a great source of repeat business and referrals.

➤ Staying in touch keeps you top-of-mind for their future needs and recommendations.

Step-by-Step Guide:

➤ **Identify Past Clients**: List clients you've worked with in the past.

➤ **Reach Out**: Send a personalized email or message to check in.

➤ **Offer Updates**: Share any new services, programs, or successes.

➤ **Invite Feedback**: Ask for their feedback and testimonials.

➤ **Propose a Follow-Up Session**: Offer a discounted or complimentary session to reconnect.

Best Practices:

➤ **Personal Touch**: Make your communication personal and relevant.

➤ **Value Proposition**: Clearly communicate the benefits of reconnecting.

Real-Life Examples:

➢ **Case Study**: Samantha followed up with past clients and secured several new coaching sessions through personalized check-ins.

Measurement and Evaluation:

➢ **Engagement Rate**: Track the response rate to your follow-up messages.

➢ **Repeat Business**: Measure the number of past clients who re-engage.

Additional Resources:

➢ **Books**: "The Referral of a Lifetime" by Tim Templeton.

➢ **Online Courses**: Life Coach Business Masterclass TransformationAcademy.com/getclients

Action Plan:

➢ **Checklist:**
   o Identify past clients.
   o Reach out with personalized messages.
   o Offer updates and invite feedback.
   o Propose follow-up sessions.

➢ **Timeline:**
   o Week 1: Identify and reach out to past clients.
   o Week 2: Offer updates and invite feedback.
   o Week 3: Propose follow-up sessions.

9. CREATE A REFERRAL PROGRAM

Introduction:

> ➤ A referral program incentivizes your clients and network to refer new clients to you.

> ➤ It's an effective way to leverage word-of-mouth marketing.

Step-by-Step Guide:

> ➤ **Define Incentives**: Decide on the rewards for successful referrals (e.g., discounts, free sessions).

> ➤ **Promote the Program**: Inform your clients and network about the referral program.

> ➤ **Track Referrals**: Use a system to track referrals and ensure rewards are given.

> ➤ **Follow Up**: Thank those who refer clients and provide updates on the results.

Best Practices:

> ➤ **Clear Guidelines**: Ensure the referral process and rewards are clearly communicated.

> ➤ **Timely Rewards**: Provide rewards promptly to maintain trust and motivation.

Real-Life Examples:

> ➤ **Case Study**: Alex implemented a referral program and saw a 20% increase in new clients within three months.

Measurement and Evaluation:

> ➤ **Number of Referrals**: Track the number of referrals received.

➢ **Conversion Rate**: Measure the percentage of referrals that convert to clients.

Additional Resources:

➢ **Books**: "Referral Engine" by John Jantsch.

➢ **Online Courses**: Life Coach Business Masterclass TransformationAcademy.com/getclients

Action Plan:

➢ **Checklist:**

o Define incentives.

o Promote the program.

o Track referrals.

o Follow up and reward.

➢ **Timeline:**

o Week 1: Define and promote the program.

10. OFFER FREE CONTENT

Introduction:

➢ Providing free content establishes your expertise and attracts potential clients.

➢ It builds trust and demonstrates the value of your coaching services.

Step-by-Step Guide:

➢ **Choose Content Types**: Decide on the types of content you'll offer (e.g., blogs, videos, podcasts).

- ➤ **Create High-Quality Content**: Develop content that addresses common challenges and provides valuable insights.
- ➤ **Distribute Content**: Share your content through your website, social media, and email newsletters.
- ➤ **Engage with Your Audience**: Encourage feedback and discussions to build a community.
- ➤ **Include a Call-to-Action**: Invite readers or viewers to take the next step, such as signing up for a consultation.

Best Practices:

- ➤ **Consistency**: Regularly publish content to keep your audience engaged.
- ➤ **Value-Focused**: Ensure your content provides actionable insights and value.

Real-Life Examples:

- ➤ **Case Study**: Rachel's blog on personal development attracted thousands of readers and converted many into paying clients through consistent, valuable content.

Measurement and Evaluation:

- ➤ **Engagement Metrics**: Track views, likes, shares, and comments.
- ➤ **Lead Generation**: Measure the number of leads generated from your content.

Additional Resources:

- ➤ **Books**: "Content Inc." by Joe Pulizzi.
- ➤ **Online Courses**: Life Coach Business Masterclass TransformationAcademy.com/getclients

Action Plan:

> ### ➢ Checklist:

- o Choose content types.
- o Create high-quality content.
- o Distribute content.
- o Engage with your audience.
- o Include a call-to-action.

> ### ➢ Timeline:

- o Week 1: Plan content strategy.
- o Ongoing: Create and publish content.
- o Week 4: Engage and evaluate results.

CHAPTER 2:
COLLABORATION AND PARTNERSHIPS

11. COLLABORATE WITH OTHER COACHES

Introduction:

➢ Partnering with other coaches can expand your reach and bring in new clients.

➢ Collaboration allows you to offer more comprehensive services and tap into each other's networks.

Step-by-Step Guide:

➢ **Identify Potential Partners**: Look for coaches in complementary niches.

➢ **Propose Collaboration**: Reach out and suggest ways you can work together (e.g., joint workshops, cross-promotion).

➢ **Plan the Collaboration**: Define the goals, roles, and responsibilities of each party.

➢ **Promote the Collaboration**: Use both networks to advertise your joint efforts.

➢ **Execute and Evaluate**: Conduct the collaboration and evaluate the outcomes.

Best Practices:

- ➤ **Mutual Benefit**: Ensure that the collaboration is beneficial for both parties.
- ➤ **Clear Communication**: Maintain open and clear communication throughout the process.

Real-Life Examples:

- ➤ **Case Study**: Amanda, a life coach, collaborated with a fitness coach to offer a holistic wellness program, attracting clients interested in both services.

Measurement and Evaluation:

- ➤ **Engagement Metrics**: Track participation and feedback.
- ➤ **Client Conversion**: Measure the number of new clients gained through the collaboration.

Additional Resources:

- ➤ **Books**: "The Art of Collaboration" by Betsy Clark.
- ➤ **Online Courses**: Life Coach Business Masterclass TransformationAcademy.com/getclients

Action Plan:

- ➤ **Checklist**:
  - o Identify partners.
  - o Propose collaboration.
  - o Plan collaboration.
  - o Promote efforts.
  - o Execute and evaluate.
- ➤ **Timeline**:
  - o Week 1: Identify and reach out to partners.
  - o Week 2: Plan the collaboration.

- Week 3: Promote and execute.
- Week 4: Evaluate results.

12. ATTEND WORKSHOPS AND SEMINARS

Introduction:

> Attending workshops and seminars keeps you updated on industry trends and allows you to network with potential clients.

Step-by-Step Guide:

> **Research Events**: Find relevant workshops and seminars.

> **Register and Prepare**: Sign up and prepare materials (e.g., business cards, elevator pitch).

> **Participate Actively**: Engage in sessions and network during breaks.

> **Follow Up**: Connect with new contacts after the event.

Best Practices:

> **Active Engagement**: Participate in discussions and ask questions.

> **Networking**: Make an effort to meet new people and exchange contact information.

Real-Life Examples:

> **Case Study**: Michael attended a business seminar and gained valuable contacts, resulting in two new clients.

Measurement and Evaluation:

> **Contacts Made**: Track the number of new contacts.

➤ **Client Conversion**: Measure how many new clients resulted from these events.

Additional Resources:

➤ **Books**: "How to Win Friends and Influence People" by Dale Carnegie.

➤ **Online Courses**: Life Coach Business Masterclass TransformationAcademy.com/getclients

Action Plan:

➤ **Checklist:**
  o Research events.
  o Register and prepare.
  o Participate actively.
  o Follow up.

➤ **Timeline:**
  o Week 1: Research and register.
  o Week 2: Prepare materials.
  o Week 3: Attend event.
  o Week 4: Follow up.

13. PROVIDE VALUE IN ONLINE FORUMS

Introduction:

➤ Online forums are a great place to share your expertise and attract potential clients.

➤ Engaging in forums builds your reputation and visibility.

Step-by-Step Guide:

➢ **Identify Relevant Forums**: Find forums related to your coaching niche (e.g., Reddit, Quora).

➢ **Create a Profile**: Set up a professional profile that highlights your expertise.

➢ **Engage Regularly**: Answer questions, participate in discussions, and share valuable content.

➢ **Promote Subtly**: Offer your services when relevant without being overly promotional.

Best Practices:

➢ **Consistency**: Engage regularly to build a presence.

➢ **Value-First Approach**: Focus on providing value rather than promoting services.

Real-Life Examples:

➢ **Case Study**: Lisa consistently answered questions on a career coaching forum and attracted several clients through her valuable advice.

Measurement and Evaluation:

➢ **Engagement Metrics**: Track posts, responses, and upvotes.

➢ **Leads Generated**: Measure the number of leads from forum engagements.

Additional Resources:

➢ **Books**: "The Lean Startup" by Eric Ries.

➢ **Online Courses**: Life Coach Business Masterclass
TransformationAcademy.com/getclients

Action Plan:

- ➤ Checklist:
  - o Identify forums.
  - o Create a profile.
  - o Engage regularly.
  - o Promote subtly.
- ➤ Timeline:
  - o Week 1: Identify and join forums.
  - o Week 2: Create a profile.
  - o Ongoing: Engage and promote.

14. RUN A SOCIAL MEDIA CONTEST

Introduction:

- ➤ Social media contests are a fun way to engage your audience and attract new clients.
- ➤ They increase visibility and can generate leads through participation.

Step-by-Step Guide:

- ➤ **Define the Contest**: Choose a contest type (e.g., photo contest, giveaway) and set the rules.
- ➤ **Promote the Contest**: Use social media platforms and your network to spread the word.
- ➤ **Engage Participants**: Interact with participants and encourage them to share the contest.
- ➤ **Announce Winners**: Select and announce the winners, providing the promised prizes.

➤ **Follow Up**: Reach out to participants and invite them to learn more about your services.

Best Practices:

➤ **Clear Rules**: Ensure the contest rules are easy to understand.

➤ **Attractive Prizes**: Offer prizes that are appealing to your target audience.

Real-Life Examples:

➤ **Case Study**: Jessica ran a social media contest offering a free coaching session as a prize, resulting in increased engagement and new clients.

Measurement and Evaluation:

➤ **Participation Metrics**: Track the number of participants and engagement.

➤ **Leads Generated**: Measure the number of leads from the contest.

Additional Resources:

➤ **Books**: "Jab, Jab, Jab, Right Hook" by Gary Vaynerchuk.

➤ **Online Courses**: Life Coach Business Masterclass TransformationAcademy.com/getclients

Action Plan:

➤ **Checklist**:
  o Define contest.
  o Promote contest.
  o Engage participants.
  o Announce winners.

o Follow up.

> **Timeline:**

o Week 1: Define and plan contest.

o Week 2: Promote contest.

o Week 3: Engage and run contest.

o Week 4: Announce winners and follow up.

15. OFFER DISCOUNTS FOR FIRST SESSIONS

Introduction:

> Offering discounts for the first coaching session can attract new clients and give them a low-risk opportunity to try your services.

Step-by-Step Guide:

> **Define the Offer**: Decide on the discount amount and conditions (e.g., first session free or 50% off).

> **Promote the Offer**: Advertise the discount through your website, social media, and email marketing.

> **Schedule Sessions**: Use a scheduling tool to manage bookings.

> **Provide Value**: Ensure the discounted session provides significant value to encourage continued coaching.

> **Follow Up**: Send a thank-you email and offer a package for ongoing sessions.

Best Practices:

> **Clear Terms**: Ensure the discount terms are clear and easy to understand.

> **Quality Service**: Deliver a high-quality session to convert clients into ongoing coaching.

Real-Life Examples:

➢ **Case Study**: David offered a 50% discount on the first session and converted 40% of participants into regular clients.

Measurement and Evaluation:

➢ **Number of Discounted Sessions**: Track the number of discounted sessions booked.

➢ **Conversion Rate**: Measure the percentage of discounted sessions that convert to ongoing clients.

Additional Resources:

➢ **Books**: "The Art of Selling Coaching" by Nikki Owen.

➢ **Online Courses**: Life Coach Business Masterclass TransformationAcademy.com/getclients

Action Plan:

➢ **Checklist:**
  o Define the offer.
  o Promote the offer.
  o Schedule sessions.
  o Provide value.
  o Follow up.

➢ **Timeline:**
  o Week 1: Define and promote the offer.
  o Ongoing: Schedule and conduct sessions.
  o Week 4: Follow up with clients.

16. DEVELOP A STRONG ONLINE PRESENCE

Introduction:

- ➤ A strong online presence helps potential clients find you and builds credibility.
- ➤ It includes a professional website, active social media profiles, and consistent branding.

Step-by-Step Guide:

- ➤ **Create a Website**: Develop a professional website that highlights your services, testimonials, and contact information.
- ➤ **Set Up Social Media Profiles**: Create profiles on platforms relevant to your audience (e.g., LinkedIn, Facebook, Instagram).
- ➤ **Consistent Branding**: Use consistent logos, colors, and messaging across all platforms.
- ➤ **Regular Updates**: Post regularly on your website and social media with valuable content.
- ➤ **Engage with Your Audience**: Respond to comments and messages promptly.

Best Practices:

- ➤ **Professional Design**: Ensure your website and profiles look professional and are easy to navigate.
- ➤ **SEO Optimization**: Optimize your website for search engines to attract organic traffic.

Real-Life Examples:

➢ **Case Study**: Emma revamped her online presence and saw a significant increase in client inquiries through her website and social media.

Measurement and Evaluation:

➢ **Website Traffic**: Track the number of visitors to your website.

➢ **Social Media Engagement**: Measure likes, shares, comments, and follows.

➢ **Leads Generated**: Track the number of leads from your online presence.

Additional Resources:

➢ **Books**: "Building a StoryBrand" by Donald Miller.

➢ **Online Courses**: Life Coach Business Masterclass TransformationAcademy.com/getclients

Action Plan:

➢ **Checklist:**
  o Create a website.
  o Set up social media profiles.
  o Ensure consistent branding.
  o Post regular updates.
  o Engage with your audience.

➢ **Timeline:**
  o Week 1: Create and set up profiles.
  o Week 2: Develop and optimize website.
  o Ongoing: Post updates and engage.

17. PUBLISH CASE STUDIES

Introduction:

➤ Case studies showcase your success stories and demonstrate the effectiveness of your coaching.

➤ They provide social proof and build credibility with potential clients.

Step-by-Step Guide:

➤ **Identify Success Stories**: Choose clients who have achieved significant results through your coaching.

➤ **Get Client Permission**: Ensure you have permission to share their story.

➤ **Write the Case Study**: Include the client's background, the challenges they faced, the coaching process, and the results achieved.

➤ **Design the Case Study**: Make it visually appealing with images, quotes, and clear formatting.

➤ **Publish and Promote**: Share the case study on your website, social media, and in your marketing materials.

Best Practices:

➤ **Detailed and Specific**: Provide specific details and measurable results.

➤ **Client Quotes**: Include quotes from the client to add authenticity.

Real-Life Examples:

- ➢ **Case Study**: John published a case study about a client who doubled their business revenue, attracting several new clients interested in similar results.

Measurement and Evaluation:

- ➢ **Engagement Metrics**: Track views, shares, and comments on the case study.
- ➢ **Leads Generated**: Measure the number of leads from the case study.

Additional Resources:

- ➢ **Books**: "Made to Stick" by Chip Heath and Dan Heath.
- ➢ **Online Courses**: Life Coach Business Masterclass TransformationAcademy.com/getclients

Action Plan:

- ➢ **Checklist:**
  - o Identify success stories.
  - o Get client permission.
  - o Write and design case study.
  - o Publish and promote.
- ➢ **Timeline:**
  - o Week 1: Identify stories and get permission.
  - o Week 2: Write and design case study.
  - o Week 3: Publish and promote.

18. HOST A PODCAST

Introduction:

> Hosting a podcast allows you to share your expertise, interview industry leaders, and attract potential clients.

> Podcasts build authority and provide valuable content to your audience.

Step-by-Step Guide:

> **Choose a Niche**: Select a specific niche or topic for your podcast that aligns with your coaching services.

> **Plan Episodes**: Outline episode topics, format, and guest speakers.

> **Set Up Equipment**: Invest in a good microphone, headphones, and recording software.

> **Record and Edit**: Record episodes and edit them for quality.

> **Publish and Promote**: Share your podcast on platforms like Apple Podcasts, Spotify, and social media.

Best Practices:

> **Consistent Schedule**: Release episodes on a regular schedule to build an audience.

> **High-Quality Content**: Ensure each episode provides value and engages listeners.

Real-Life Examples:

> **Case Study**: Sarah's career coaching podcast attracted thousands of listeners, many of whom became clients.

Measurement and Evaluation:

➤ **Download Metrics**: Track the number of downloads and listens.

➤ **Engagement Metrics**: Measure listener engagement through reviews and social media interactions.

Additional Resources:

➤ **Books**: "Podcasting for Dummies" by Tee Morris and Chuck Tomasi.

➤ **Online Courses**: Life Coach Business Masterclass TransformationAcademy.com/getclients

Action Plan:

➤ **Checklist:**

- o Choose a niche.
- o Plan episodes.
- o Set up equipment.
- o Record and edit episodes.
- o Publish and promote.

➤ **Timeline:**

- o Week 1: Plan and prepare.
- o Week 2: Record and edit episodes.
- o Week 3: Publish and promote.
- o Ongoing: Release new episodes regularly.

19. CREATE A YOUTUBE CHANNEL

Introduction:

> A YouTube channel allows you to share video content, tutorials, and client success stories.

> Videos can attract a wide audience and showcase your expertise visually.

Step-by-Step Guide:

> **Set Up the Channel**: Create a YouTube channel with a professional name and branding.

> **Plan Content**: Outline video topics that are relevant to your coaching services.

> **Invest in Equipment**: Use a good camera, microphone, and editing software.

> **Create and Upload Videos**: Film high-quality videos and upload them to your channel.

> **Promote Your Channel**: Share your videos on social media and embed them on your website.

Best Practices:

> **Consistency**: Upload videos regularly to build an audience.

> **Engagement**: Encourage viewers to like, comment, and subscribe.

Real-Life Examples:

> **Case Study**: Matt's fitness coaching YouTube channel grew rapidly, bringing in new clients through his engaging workout videos.

Measurement and Evaluation:

- ➤ **View Metrics**: Track views, likes, and shares.
- ➤ **Subscriber Growth**: Measure the growth of your subscriber base.
- ➤ **Leads Generated**: Track the number of leads from your YouTube channel.

Additional Resources:

- ➤ **Books**: "YouTube Secrets" by Sean Cannell and Benji Travis.

Action Plan:

- ➤ **Checklist:**
  - o Set up the channel.
  - o Plan content.
  - o Invest in equipment.
  - o Create and upload videos.
  - o Promote your channel.
- ➤ **Timeline:**
  - o Week 1: Set up and plan.
  - o Week 2: Create and upload initial videos.
  - o Ongoing: Upload and promote regularly.

20. SEND PERSONALIZED EMAILS

Introduction:

- ➤ Personalized emails can engage potential clients and build relationships.
- ➤ They show that you care about their specific needs and are not just sending generic messages.

Step-by-Step Guide:

- ➢ **Build an Email List**: Collect email addresses from your website, social media, and networking events.
- ➢ **Segment Your List**: Organize your list based on interests, demographics, and behaviors.
- ➢ **Craft Personalized Messages**: Write emails that address the recipient's specific needs and challenges.
- ➢ **Automate Follow-Ups**: Use email marketing tools to automate personalized follow-ups.
- ➢ **Track Engagement**: Monitor open rates, click-through rates, and responses.

Best Practices:

- ➢ **Personal Touch**: Use the recipient's name and reference their specific needs.
- ➢ **Value-Driven Content**: Provide valuable information and resources in your emails.

Real-Life Examples:

- ➢ **Case Study**: Chris personalized his email campaigns and saw a significant increase in client engagement and conversions.

Measurement and Evaluation:

- ➢ **Open Rates**: Track the percentage of emails opened.
- ➢ **Click-Through Rates**: Measure the percentage of clicks on links in your emails.
- ➢ **Conversion Rates**: Track the percentage of email recipients who become clients.

Additional Resources:

- ➢ **Books**: "Email Marketing Rules" by Chad S. White.

➢ **Online Courses**: Email Marketing Campaigns a Complete Guide <u>TransformationAcademy.com/getclientsem</u>

Action Plan:

➢ **Checklist:**
  - o Build and segment your list.
  - o Craft personalized messages.
  - o Automate follow-ups.
  - o Track engagement.

➢ **Timeline:**
  - o Week 1: Build and segment the list.
  - o Week 2: Craft and send initial emails.
  - o Ongoing: Automate follow-ups and track results.

CHAPTER 3:
ADVERTISING AND PUBLIC RELATIONS

21. ADVERTISE ON SOCIAL MEDIA

Introduction:

➢ Social media advertising allows you to reach a targeted audience and attract potential clients.

➢ Platforms like Facebook, Instagram, and LinkedIn offer robust advertising tools.

Step-by-Step Guide:

➢ **Choose a Platform**: Select the social media platform(s) most relevant to your audience.

➢ **Define Your Goals**: Set clear objectives for your ad campaign (e.g., brand awareness, lead generation).

➢ **Create Ad Content**: Design eye-catching ads with compelling copy and visuals.

➢ **Set a Budget**: Determine how much you're willing to spend on the campaign.

➢ **Target Your Audience**: Use demographic and interest-based targeting to reach the right people.

➤ **Monitor and Optimize**: Track the performance of your ads and adjust as needed for better results.

Best Practices:

➤ **A/B Testing**: Test different ad variations to see what works best.

➤ **Clear Call-to-Action**: Ensure your ads have a clear and compelling call-to-action.

Real-Life Examples:

➤ **Case Study**: Julie ran a targeted Facebook ad campaign that resulted in a 25% increase in new client inquiries.

Measurement and Evaluation:

➤ **Impressions and Reach**: Track how many people saw your ads.

➤ **Click-Through Rate (CTR)**: Measure the percentage of people who clicked on your ad.

➤ **Conversion Rate**: Track the percentage of clicks that lead to client inquiries or sign-ups.

Additional Resources:

➤ **Books**: "Killer Facebook Ads" by Marty Weintraub.

Action Plan:

➤ **Checklist:**
   o Choose platform.
   o Define goals.
   o Create ad content.
   o Set budget.
   o Target audience.
   o Monitor and optimize.

> **Timeline:**
> - o Week 1: Choose platform and define goals.
> - o Week 2: Create content and set budget.
> - o Ongoing: Launch, monitor, and optimize campaign.
> - o Ongoing: Track referrals and provide rewards.
> - o Week 4: Follow up and evaluate results.

22. PARTICIPATE IN ONLINE CHALLENGES

Introduction:

> - Online challenges engage your audience and attract potential clients by providing valuable content and interaction.
> - They are a fun way to showcase your expertise and build a community.

Step-by-Step Guide:

> - **Define the Challenge**: Choose a relevant topic and set the duration (e.g., 7-day fitness challenge).
> - **Create a Schedule**: Outline daily tasks or activities for participants.
> - **Promote the Challenge**: Use social media, email marketing, and your website to promote the challenge.
> - **Engage Participants**: Interact with participants through live sessions, Q&A, and support.
> - **Provide Value**: Offer tips, resources, and motivation throughout the challenge.
> - **Follow Up**: After the challenge, reach out to participants with a special offer for your coaching services.

Best Practices:

➢ **Interactive Elements**: Include live sessions, group activities, and daily check-ins.

➢ **Clear Instructions**: Provide clear and concise instructions for each day's activity.

Real-Life Examples:

➢ **Case Study**: Anna ran a 30-day mindfulness challenge and gained several new clients who were impressed with her daily tips and support.

Measurement and Evaluation:

➢ **Participation Rate**: Track the number of participants who join the challenge.

➢ **Engagement Levels**: Measure engagement through comments, likes, and shares.

➢ **Conversion Rate**: Track the number of participants who become clients.

Additional Resources:

➢ **Books**: "Challenge Accepted!" by Mary Ann Casey.

Action Plan:

➢ **Checklist:**
  o Define the challenge.
  o Create a schedule.
  o Promote the challenge.
  o Engage participants.
  o Provide value.
  o Follow up.

> **Timeline:**
> - Week 1: Define and plan the challenge.
> - Week 2: Promote the challenge.
> - Week 3: Run the challenge.
> - Week 4: Follow up with participants.

23. OFFER GROUP COACHING SESSIONS

Introduction:

> - Group coaching sessions allow you to reach multiple clients at once, providing a more affordable option for participants and maximizing your time.
> - They create a supportive community where clients can learn from each other.

Step-by-Step Guide:

> - **Define the Group**: Choose a specific topic or goal for the group coaching sessions.
> - **Set a Schedule**: Decide on the frequency and duration of the sessions (e.g., weekly for 6 weeks).
> - **Create Content**: Develop a structured program with specific outcomes for each session.
> - **Promote the Group**: Advertise the group coaching program through your website, social media, and email marketing.
> - **Facilitate Sessions**: Lead the sessions, ensuring each participant has a chance to contribute.
> - **Follow Up**: Provide additional resources and support between sessions.

Best Practices:

- ➢ **Interactive Format**: Encourage discussion, Q&A, and peer support.
- ➢ **Clear Agenda**: Have a clear agenda and goals for each session.

Real-Life Examples:

- ➢ **Case Study**: Mark's group coaching program on business growth helped participants increase their revenue, and many continued with one-on-one coaching afterward.

Measurement and Evaluation:

- ➢ **Participation Rate**: Track the number of participants.
- ➢ **Engagement Levels**: Measure engagement during sessions through participation and feedback.
- ➢ **Client Conversion**: Track the number of group participants who transition to one-on-one coaching.

Additional Resources:

- ➢ **Books**: "The Art of Group Coaching" by Jennifer Britton.
- ➢ **Online Courses**: Group Life Coach Certification TransformationAcademy.com/getclientsgroup

Action Plan:

- ➢ **Checklist:**
  - o Define the group.
  - o Set a schedule.
  - o Create content.
  - o Promote the group.
  - o Facilitate sessions.
  - o Follow up.

> **Timeline:**
>   o Week 1: Plan and create content.
>   o Week 2: Promote the group.
>   o Week 3: Start sessions.
>   o Ongoing: Facilitate and follow up.

24. FOLLOW UP WITH LEADS

Introduction:

> Consistent follow-up with leads is crucial for converting prospects into clients.

> It shows that you're interested and invested in their needs and progress.

Step-by-Step Guide:

> **Organize Leads**: Use a CRM tool to manage and track your leads.

> **Schedule Follow-Ups**: Set reminders to follow up with leads regularly.

> **Personalize Communication**: Tailor your follow-up messages to address the lead's specific needs and interests.

> **Provide Value**: Share useful content, resources, or offers in your follow-up emails.

> **Ask for Feedback**: Invite leads to share their thoughts or ask questions to keep the conversation going.

> **Invite to Action**: Include a clear call-to-action, such as scheduling a consultation or signing up for a program.

Best Practices:

- ➢ **Consistency**: Follow up regularly without being too pushy.
- ➢ **Value-Focused**: Ensure each follow-up provides value to the lead.

Real-Life Examples:

- ➢ **Case Study**: Lisa's consistent follow-up strategy increased her client conversion rate by 30%.

Measurement and Evaluation:

- ➢ **Response Rate**: Track the percentage of leads who respond to follow-ups.
- ➢ **Conversion Rate**: Measure the percentage of leads who become clients.
- ➢ **Engagement Metrics**: Monitor open and click-through rates of follow-up emails.

Additional Resources:

- ➢ **Books**: "Follow Up and Close the Sale" by Jeff Shore.
- ➢ **Online Courses**: Life Coach Business Masterclass TransformationAcademy.com/getclients

Action Plan:

- ➢ **Checklist:**
  - o Organize leads.
  - o Schedule follow-ups.
  - o Personalize communication.
  - o Provide value.
  - o Ask for feedback.
  - o Invite to action.

➤ **Timeline:**
  - ○ Week 1: Organize and schedule.
  - ○ Ongoing: Follow up and track results.

25. CREATE AN ENGAGING NEWSLETTER

Introduction:

➤ An engaging newsletter keeps you top-of-mind with potential and existing clients.

➤ It provides valuable content, updates, and offers directly to their inbox.

Step-by-Step Guide:

➤ **Build a Subscriber List**: Collect email addresses through your website, social media, and events.

➤ **Plan Content**: Decide on the content types and frequency of your newsletter.

➤ **Design the Newsletter**: Use email marketing tools to create a visually appealing layout.

➤ **Write Engaging Content**: Include valuable tips, success stories, and upcoming events.

➤ **Include a Call-to-Action**: Encourage readers to take action, such as booking a session or visiting your website.

➤ **Analyze Performance**: Track open rates, click-through rates, and conversions.

Best Practices:

➤ **Consistency**: Send newsletters regularly (e.g., weekly, bi-weekly, monthly).

➤ **Value-Driven Content**: Ensure each newsletter provides value to the reader.

Real-Life Examples:

➢ **Case Study**: Robert's monthly newsletter increased his website traffic and client inquiries by 20%.

Measurement and Evaluation:

➢ **Open Rates**: Track the percentage of subscribers who open your emails.

➢ **Click-Through Rates**: Measure the percentage of clicks on links in your emails.

➢ **Conversions**: Track the number of leads and clients from the newsletter.

Additional Resources:

➢ **Books**: "The New Email Revolution" by Robert W. Bly.

Action Plan:

➢ **Checklist:**
  o Build a subscriber list.
  o Plan content.
  o Design the newsletter.
  o Write engaging content.
  o Include a call-to-action.
  o Analyze performance.

➢ **Timeline:**
  o Week 1: Build list and plan content.
  o Week 2: Design and write the newsletter.
  o Ongoing: Send and analyze.

26. WRITE A BOOK OR EBOOK

Introduction:

➤ Writing a book or eBook establishes you as an authority in your field and provides a valuable resource for potential clients.

➤ It can attract clients through book sales, lead magnets, and increased credibility.

Step-by-Step Guide:

➤ **Choose a Topic**: Select a topic that aligns with your coaching services and addresses a common client need.

➤ **Outline the Content**: Plan the structure and key points of your book.

➤ **Write the Book**: Dedicate regular time to writing and complete each chapter.

➤ **Edit and Proofread**: Ensure your book is polished and professional.

➤ **Design the Cover**: Create an attractive cover that reflects the content.

➤ **Publish and Promote**: Use self-publishing platforms like Amazon Kindle and promote through your network.

Best Practices:

➤ **Professional Editing**: Hire a professional editor to ensure quality.

➤ **Consistent Writing Schedule**: Set aside regular time for writing to stay on track.

Real-Life Examples:

➤ **Case Study**: Tom's self-help eBook became a bestseller on Amazon, leading to numerous coaching inquiries.

Measurement and Evaluation:

➤ **Sales Metrics**: Track the number of books sold.

➤ **Lead Generation**: Measure the number of leads generated from book promotions.

Additional Resources:

➤ **Books**: "How to Write a Book Proposal" by Michael Larsen.

➤ **Online Course:** Writing Your Masterpiece
TransformationAcademy.com/getclientswm

Action Plan:

➤ **Checklist:**
  o Choose a topic.
  o Outline content.
  o Write the book.
  o Edit and proofread.
  o Design cover.
  o Publish and promote.

➤ **Timeline:**
  o Week 1: Choose topic and outline.
  o Ongoing: Write, edit, and design.
  o Week 8: Publish and promote.

27. OFFER WEBINARS ON SPECIFIC TOPICS

Introduction:

➤ Webinars allow you to share your expertise on specific topics and engage with a broad audience.

➤ They provide valuable content and can lead to new client inquiries.

Step-by-Step Guide:

➤ **Choose a Topic**: Select a relevant and engaging topic that addresses common client needs.

➤ **Plan the Webinar**: Outline the content, structure, and key takeaways.

➤ **Set a Date and Time**: Choose a convenient time for your target audience.

➤ **Promote the Webinar**: Use social media, email marketing, and your network to spread the word.

➤ **Prepare Materials**: Create slides, handouts, and other resources.

➤ **Host the Webinar**: Engage with participants, encourage questions, and provide actionable insights.

➤ **Follow Up**: Send a thank-you email with a summary of the webinar and additional resources.

Best Practices:

➤ **Interactive Elements**: Incorporate Q&A sessions, polls, and live demonstrations.

➤ **Clear Value Proposition**: Ensure participants understand the benefits they'll gain.

Real-Life Examples:

- ➤ **Case Study**: Emma's webinar on career advancement attracted hundreds of attendees, many of whom signed up for her coaching services.

Measurement and Evaluation:

- ➤ **Attendance Numbers**: Track the number of participants.
- ➤ **Engagement Levels**: Measure engagement through participation and feedback.
- ➤ **Conversion Rate**: Track the percentage of attendees who become clients.

Additional Resources:

- ➤ **Books**: "Webinars That Convert" by Lewis Howes.
- ➤ **Online Courses**: Life Coach Business Masterclass TransformationAcademy.com/getclients

Action Plan:

- ➤ **Checklist:**
  - o Choose a topic.
  - o Plan the webinar.
  - o Set date and time.
  - o Promote the webinar.
  - o Prepare materials.
  - o Host the webinar.
  - o Follow up.
- ➤ **Timeline:**
  - o Week 1: Choose topic and plan content.
  - o Week 2: Promote webinar.
  - o Week 3: Finalize preparations.

○ Week 4: Host and follow up.

28. USE TESTIMONIALS EFFECTIVELY

Introduction:

➤ Client testimonials provide social proof and build trust with potential clients.

➤ They showcase the positive experiences and results of your past clients.

Step-by-Step Guide:

➤ **Collect Testimonials**: Ask satisfied clients for written or video testimonials.

➤ **Highlight Key Points**: Focus on specific results and benefits clients have experienced.

➤ **Display Prominently**: Feature testimonials on your website, social media, and marketing materials.

➤ **Use Various Formats**: Include text, video, and audio testimonials to appeal to different audiences.

➤ **Regularly Update**: Keep your testimonials fresh and relevant by adding new ones regularly.

Best Practices:

➤ **Authenticity**: Ensure testimonials are genuine and specific.

➤ **Diverse Perspectives**: Include testimonials from a variety of clients to show broad appeal.

Real-Life Examples:

➤ **Case Study**: Sarah's use of video testimonials on her website increased her client inquiries by 35%.

Measurement and Evaluation:

- ➤ **Engagement Metrics**: Track views, likes, and shares of testimonials.
- ➤ **Lead Generation**: Measure the number of leads generated from testimonial pages.

Additional Resources:

- ➤ **Books**: "The Power of Testimonials" by John Smith.

Action Plan:

- ➤ **Checklist:**
  - o Collect testimonials.
  - o Highlight key points.
  - o Display prominently.
  - o Use various formats.
  - o Regularly update.
- ➤ **Timeline:**
  - o Week 1: Collect and highlight testimonials.
  - o Ongoing: Display and update regularly.

29. RUN PAID SEARCH CAMPAIGNS

Introduction:

- ➤ Paid search campaigns allow you to target potential clients actively searching for your services.
- ➤ Platforms like Google Ads offer tools to create and manage effective search campaigns.

Step-by-Step Guide:

- ➤ **Choose Keywords**: Select relevant keywords that your target audience is likely to search.
- ➤ **Create Ad Copy**: Write compelling ad copy that includes a strong call-to-action.
- ➤ **Set a Budget**: Determine your daily or monthly budget for the campaign.
- ➤ **Target Your Audience**: Use demographic and geographic targeting to reach the right people.
- ➤ **Launch the Campaign**: Set up and launch your ads on the chosen platform.
- ➤ **Monitor and Optimize**: Track the performance of your ads and make adjustments as needed.

Best Practices:

- ➤ **Keyword Research**: Use tools like Google Keyword Planner to find effective keywords.
- ➤ **A/B Testing**: Test different ad variations to see what works best.

Real-Life Examples:

- ➤ **Case Study**: David's Google Ads campaign targeting "business coaching" resulted in a significant increase in client inquiries.

Measurement and Evaluation:

- ➤ **Impressions and Clicks**: Track the number of impressions and clicks.
- ➤ **Click-Through Rate (CTR)**: Measure the percentage of clicks on your ads.

➤ **Conversion Rate**: Track the percentage of clicks that lead to client inquiries or sign-ups.

Additional Resources:

➤ **Books**: "Ultimate Guide to Google AdWords" by Perry Marshall.

Action Plan:

➤ **Checklist:**
  o Choose keywords.
  o Create ad copy.
  o Set a budget.
  o Target audience.
  o Launch the campaign.
  o Monitor and optimize.

➤ **Timeline:**
  o Week 1: Choose keywords and create ad copy.
  o Week 2: Set budget and target audience.
  o Week 3: Launch campaign.
  o Ongoing: Monitor and optimize.

30. DEVELOP AN ONLINE COURSE

Introduction:

➤ Creating an online course allows you to share your expertise and attract clients on a larger scale.

➤ Courses provide valuable content and can generate passive income.

Step-by-Step Guide:

- ➤ **Choose a Topic**: Select a topic that aligns with your coaching services and addresses a common client need.
- ➤ **Outline the Course**: Plan the structure and key points of your course.
- ➤ **Create Content**: Develop videos, worksheets, and other materials.
- ➤ **Choose a Platform**: Use platforms like Teachable, Udemy, or your website to host the course.
- ➤ **Promote the Course**: Advertise your course through your website, social media, and email marketing.
- ➤ **Engage with Students**: Provide support and feedback to students as they go through the course.

Best Practices:

- ➤ **High-Quality Content**: Ensure your videos and materials are professional and engaging.
- ➤ **Interactive Elements**: Include quizzes, assignments, and discussion forums to enhance learning.

Real-Life Examples:

- ➤ **Case Study**: Maria's online course on time management became a bestseller on Udemy, leading to numerous coaching inquiries.

Measurement and Evaluation:

- ➤ **Enrollment Numbers**: Track the number of students who enroll.

➢ **Completion Rate**: Measure the percentage of students who complete the course.

➢ **Lead Generation**: Track the number of leads generated from the course.

Additional Resources:

➢ **Books**: "Teach and Grow Rich" by Danny Iny.

➢ **Online Courses**: Online Course Revolution TransformationAcademy.com/getclientsoc

Action Plan:

➢ **Checklist:**

- o Choose a topic.
- o Outline the course.
- o Create content.
- o Choose a platform.
- o Promote the course.
- o Engage with students.

➢ **Timeline:**

- o Week 1: Plan and outline the course.
- o Week 2: Create content.
- o Week 3: Choose platform and upload.
- o Week 4: Promote and engage.

CHAPTER 4:
DIGITAL MARKETING AND AUTOMATION

31. HOST LIVE Q&A SESSIONS

Introduction:

➢ Hosting live Q&A sessions allows you to interact directly with potential clients and address their specific questions and concerns.

➢ It demonstrates your expertise and builds trust with your audience.

Step-by-Step Guide:

➢ **Choose a Platform**: Select a platform for your live session (e.g., Facebook Live, Instagram Live, Zoom).

➢ **Set a Date and Time**: Choose a convenient time for your target audience.

➢ **Promote the Session**: Use social media, email marketing, and your website to announce the event.

➢ **Prepare Content**: Outline key points and potential questions to address during the session.

- ➢ **Engage with Participants**: Answer questions, provide insights, and interact with attendees.
- ➢ **Follow Up**: Send a thank-you message and additional resources to participants.

Best Practices:

- ➢ **Interactive Format**: Encourage questions and participation throughout the session.
- ➢ **Clear Value Proposition**: Ensure participants know what they will gain from attending.

Real-Life Examples:

- ➢ **Case Study**: Kevin hosted a live Q&A on LinkedIn and attracted several new clients who appreciated his expertise and responsiveness.

Measurement and Evaluation:

- ➢ **Attendance Numbers**: Track the number of participants.
- ➢ **Engagement Levels**: Measure engagement through comments, questions, and interactions.
- ➢ **Conversion Rate**: Track the percentage of attendees who become clients.

Additional Resources:

- ➢ **Books**: "The Art of Virtual Facilitation" by Jason Sweet.
- ➢ **Online Courses**: Life Coach Business Masterclass TransformationAcademy.com/getclients

Action Plan:

- ➢ **Checklist:**

o Choose a platform.

o Set date and time.

o Promote the session.

o Prepare content.

o Engage with participants.

o Follow up.

➢ **Timeline:**

o Week 1: Choose platform and set date.

o Week 2: Promote and prepare content.

o Week 3: Host and follow up.

32. PARTNER WITH LOCAL BUSINESSES

Introduction:

➢ Partnering with local businesses can expand your reach and attract new clients.

➢ It allows you to offer your services to their employees or customers.

Step-by-Step Guide:

➢ **Identify Potential Partners**: Look for local businesses that align with your coaching services.

➢ **Propose Collaboration**: Reach out and suggest ways to collaborate (e.g., workshops, employee coaching).

➢ **Define Terms**: Agree on the terms of the partnership, including any fees or revenue sharing.

➢ **Promote the Partnership**: Use both your networks to promote the collaboration.

➢ **Execute and Evaluate**: Conduct the collaboration and evaluate the outcomes.

Best Practices:

- ➤ **Mutual Benefit**: Ensure that the partnership is beneficial for both parties.
- ➤ **Clear Communication**: Maintain open and clear communication throughout the process.

Real-Life Examples:

- ➤ **Case Study**: Lauren partnered with a local gym to offer wellness coaching to their members, resulting in increased clients and visibility.

Measurement and Evaluation:

- ➤ **Engagement Metrics**: Track participation and feedback.
- ➤ **Client Conversion**: Measure the number of new clients gained through the partnership.

Additional Resources:

- ➤ **Books**: "The Power of Partnership" by Riane Eisler.
- ➤ **Online Courses**: Life Coach Business Masterclass uls

Action Plan:

- ➤ **Checklist:**
  - o Identify partners.
  - o Propose collaboration.
  - o Define terms.
  - o Promote partnership.
  - o Execute and evaluate.
- ➤ **Timeline:**
  - o Week 1: Identify and reach out to partners.
  - o Week 2: Define terms and promote.
  - o Week 3: Execute and evaluate.

33. Get Featured in Media

Introduction:

➢ Being featured in media outlets increases your visibility and credibility.

➢ It positions you as an expert in your field.

Step-by-Step Guide:

➢ **Identify Media Outlets**: Look for local newspapers, magazines, blogs, and podcasts relevant to your niche.

➢ **Create a Pitch**: Write a compelling pitch that highlights your expertise and why you should be featured.

➢ **Reach Out**: Contact journalists, editors, or podcast hosts with your pitch.

➢ **Provide Value**: Offer insights, tips, or a unique perspective that would interest their audience.

➢ **Follow Up**: Keep in touch and offer additional information or interviews as needed.

Best Practices:

➢ **Tailored Pitch**: Customize your pitch for each media outlet.

➢ **Professionalism**: Maintain a professional and courteous tone in all communications.

Real-Life Examples:

➢ **Case Study**: Olivia's feature in a popular blog led to a significant increase in traffic to her website and new client inquiries.

Measurement and Evaluation:

- ➢ **Media Coverage**: Track the number of media features.
- ➢ **Engagement Metrics**: Measure the impact through website traffic, social media mentions, and inquiries.
- ➢ **Client Conversion**: Track the number of new clients gained from media exposure.

Additional Resources:

- ➢ **Books**: "Free Publicity" by Jeff Crilley.

Action Plan:

- ➢ **Checklist:**
  - o Identify media outlets.
  - o Create a pitch.
  - o Reach out.
  - o Provide value.
  - o Follow up.
- ➢ **Timeline:**
  - o Week 1: Identify outlets and create pitch.
  - o Week 2: Reach out and follow up.
  - o Ongoing: Track and evaluate results.

34. LEVERAGE SEO STRATEGIES

Introduction:

- ➢ Search Engine Optimization (SEO) improves your website's visibility on search engines, attracting organic traffic and potential clients.
- ➢ It involves optimizing your content and website structure.

Step-by-Step Guide:

- ➢ **Conduct Keyword Research**: Identify relevant keywords that your target audience is searching for.

- ➢ **Optimize Website Content**: Use these keywords in your website's content, including headings, meta descriptions, and images.

- ➢ **Create Quality Content**: Regularly publish valuable and relevant content (e.g., blog posts, videos).

- ➢ **Improve Website Structure**: Ensure your website is user-friendly and mobile-responsive.

- ➢ **Build Backlinks**: Get other reputable websites to link to your content.

Best Practices:

- ➢ **Consistency**: Regularly update and add new content.

- ➢ **Analytics**: Use tools like Google Analytics to track performance and make data-driven decisions.

Real-Life Examples:

- ➢ **Case Study**: Alex's investment in SEO strategies led to a 50% increase in website traffic and a steady stream of new clients.

Measurement and Evaluation:

- ➢ **Traffic Metrics**: Track website visits and sources of traffic.

- ➢ **Keyword Rankings**: Monitor your rankings for targeted keywords.

- ➢ **Conversion Rate**: Track the number of website visitors who become clients.

Additional Resources:

➢ **Books**: "SEO 2021" by Adam Clarke.

Action Plan:

➢ **Checklist:**

o Conduct keyword research.

o Optimize content.

o Create quality content.

o Improve website structure.

o Build backlinks.

➢ **Timeline:**

o Week 1: Conduct research and optimize content.

o Ongoing: Publish content and build backlinks.

o Week 4: Track and analyze performance.

35. ATTEND VIRTUAL SUMMITS

Introduction:

➢ Virtual summits provide opportunities to learn, network, and promote your services to a broad audience.

➢ They are cost-effective and convenient compared to in-person events.

Step-by-Step Guide:

➢ **Research Summits**: Identify virtual summits relevant to your niche.

➢ **Register and Prepare**: Sign up and prepare your materials (e.g., business cards, elevator pitch).

➢ **Participate Actively**: Engage in sessions, join discussions, and network with other attendees.

➢ **Follow Up**: Connect with new contacts after the event and explore potential collaborations or client opportunities.

Best Practices:

➢ **Engagement**: Actively participate in sessions and discussions to maximize networking opportunities.

➢ **Professionalism**: Maintain a professional demeanor throughout the event.

Real-Life Examples:

➢ **Case Study**: Rachel attended a virtual summit on leadership and gained several new clients through her active participation and follow-ups.

Measurement and Evaluation:

➢ **Connections Made**: Track the number of new contacts.

➢ **Engagement Levels**: Measure participation and interaction during the summit.

➢ **Client Conversion**: Track the number of new clients from the event.

Additional Resources:

➢ **Books**: "Virtual Summit Success" by Milana Leshinsky.

Action Plan:

➢ **Checklist:**
   o Research summits.
   o Register and prepare.
   o Participate actively.
   o Follow up.

> **Timeline:**
> - o Week 1: Research and register.
> - o Week 2: Prepare materials.
> - o Week 3: Attend summit.
> - o Week 4: Follow up.

36. CREATE ENGAGING LEAD MAGNETS

Introduction:

> Lead magnets attract potential clients by offering valuable content in exchange for their contact information.

> They help build your email list and nurture leads.

Step-by-Step Guide:

> **Choose a Lead Magnet Type**: Decide on the type of lead magnet (e.g., eBook, checklist, webinar).

> **Create Valuable Content**: Develop high-quality and relevant content that addresses a specific need or problem.

> **Design an Opt-In Form**: Create a form to capture leads' contact information.

> **Promote the Lead Magnet**: Use your website, social media, and email marketing to promote it.

> **Follow Up**: Send a thank-you email and provide additional resources or offers.

Best Practices:

> **Clear Value Proposition**: Ensure the lead magnet offers clear and valuable benefits.

> **Professional Design**: Make the lead magnet visually appealing and easy to consume.

Real-Life Examples:

➤ **Case Study**: John created a productivity checklist that significantly increased his email list and led to new client inquiries.

Measurement and Evaluation:

➤ **Opt-In Rate**: Track the number of people who download the lead magnet.

➤ **Engagement Metrics**: Measure interactions with the lead magnet (e.g., open rates, click-through rates).

➤ **Lead Conversion**: Track the number of leads who become clients.

Additional Resources:

➤ **Books**: "Lead Magnets" by Amy Porterfield.

Action Plan:

➤ **Checklist:**
- o Choose lead magnet type.
- o Create valuable content.
- o Design opt-in form.
- o Promote the lead magnet.
- o Follow up.

➤ **Timeline:**
- o Week 1: Choose type and create content.
- o Week 2: Design and promote.
- o Ongoing: Follow up and track results.

37. USE RETARGETING ADS

Introduction:

> ➢ Retargeting ads re-engage visitors who have previously visited your website but didn't convert.

> ➢ They remind potential clients of your services and encourage them to return.

Step-by-Step Guide:

> ➢ **Set Up Retargeting Pixels**: Install retargeting pixels on your website from platforms like Facebook and Google.

> ➢ **Create Retargeting Ads**: Design ads that remind visitors of your services and encourage them to take action.

> ➢ **Define Your Audience**: Target visitors who have interacted with specific pages or actions on your website.

> ➢ **Set a Budget**: Determine your daily or monthly budget for retargeting ads.

> ➢ **Launch the Campaign**: Set up and launch your retargeting ads.

> ➢ **Monitor and Optimize**: Track the performance of your ads and make adjustments as needed.

Best Practices:

> ➢ **Compelling Ads**: Create ads with strong visuals and clear calls-to-action.

> ➢ **Frequency Caps**: Set frequency caps to avoid overexposing your ads to the same audience.

Real-Life Examples:

> **Case Study**: Emily's use of retargeting ads increased her client conversions by 40%.

Measurement and Evaluation:

> **Impressions and Clicks**: Track the number of impressions and clicks.

> **Click-Through Rate (CTR)**: Measure the percentage of clicks on your ads.

> **Conversion Rate**: Track the percentage of clicks that lead to client inquiries or sign-ups.

Additional Resources:

> **Books**: "Ultimate Guide to Google AdWords" by Perry Marshall.

Action Plan:

> **Checklist:**
> - Set up retargeting pixels.
> - Create retargeting ads.
> - Define audience.
> - Set budget.
> - Launch the campaign.
> - Monitor and optimize.

> **Timeline:**
> - Week 1: Set up pixels and create ads.
> - Week 2: Define audience and set budget.
> - Week 3: Launch and monitor.

38. DEVELOP A MOBILE APP

Introduction:

➤ A mobile app can provide value and convenience to your clients, allowing them to access your services and resources on-the-go.

➤ It helps maintain engagement and provides a unique user experience.

Step-by-Step Guide:

➤ **Identify App Features**: Decide on the features your app will include (e.g., booking sessions, accessing content, notifications).

➤ **Choose a Development Platform**: Select a platform for developing your app (e.g., iOS, Android, or both).

➤ **Design the App**: Create a user-friendly and visually appealing design.

➤ **Develop the App**: Work with a developer or use app-building tools to create the app.

➤ **Test the App**: Ensure the app works smoothly and fix any issues.

➤ **Launch and Promote**: Publish the app on app stores and promote it to your clients.

Best Practices:

➤ **User Experience**: Focus on creating an intuitive and seamless user experience.

➤ **Regular Updates**: Keep the app updated with new features and improvements.

Real-Life Examples:

➢ **Case Study**: Paul developed a mobile app for his coaching business, which significantly increased client engagement and bookings.

Measurement and Evaluation:

➢ **Download Metrics**: Track the number of downloads and installations.

➢ **User Engagement**: Measure how frequently users interact with the app.

➢ **Client Conversion**: Track the number of app users who become clients.

Additional Resources:

➢ **Books**: "App Empire" by Chad Mureta.

Action Plan:

➢ **Checklist:**
  o Identify app features.
  o Choose development platform.
  o Design the app.
  o Develop the app.
  o Test the app.
  o Launch and promote.
➢ **Timeline:**
  o Week 1: Plan features and design.
  o Week 2: Develop and test.
  o Week 3: Launch and promote.

39. OFFER A MONEY-BACK GUARANTEE

Introduction:

➢ A money-back guarantee reduces the risk for new clients and can increase trust and conversions.

➢ It demonstrates confidence in your services and commitment to client satisfaction.

Step-by-Step Guide:

➢ **Define the Guarantee**: Decide on the terms of the guarantee (e.g., 30-day satisfaction guarantee).

➢ **Communicate Clearly**: Clearly state the guarantee on your website and marketing materials.

➢ **Set Up a Process**: Establish a process for handling refund requests.

➢ **Promote the Guarantee**: Highlight the guarantee in your promotions to attract new clients.

➢ **Monitor Feedback**: Collect feedback from clients to improve your services and reduce refund requests.

Best Practices:

➢ **Clear Terms**: Ensure the terms of the guarantee are easy to understand.

➢ **Responsive Service**: Respond promptly to refund requests and feedback.

Real-Life Examples:

➢ **Case Study**: Michelle's money-back guarantee led to a 20% increase in client sign-ups, with very few refund requests due to high satisfaction.

Measurement and Evaluation:

- ➤ **Conversion Rate**: Track the increase in new client sign-ups.
- ➤ **Refund Requests**: Measure the number of refund requests and reasons.
- ➤ **Client Feedback**: Collect and analyze feedback from clients.

Additional Resources:

- ➤ **Books**: "The Trusted Advisor" by David H. Maister.

Action Plan:

- ➤ **Checklist:**
  - ○ Define the guarantee.
  - ○ Communicate clearly.
  - ○ Set up a process.
  - ○ Promote the guarantee.
  - ○ Monitor feedback.
- ➤ **Timeline:**
  - ○ Week 1: Define terms and set up process.
  - ○ Week 2: Communicate and promote.
  - ○ Ongoing: Monitor and respond to feedback.

40. CONDUCT MARKET RESEARCH

Introduction:

- ➤ Market research helps you understand your target audience, their needs, and preferences, allowing you to tailor your services and marketing strategies effectively.
- ➤ It provides insights into market trends and competitor strategies.

Step-by-Step Guide:

➢ **Define Objectives**: Determine what you want to learn from your market research.

➢ **Choose Research Methods**: Select methods such as surveys, interviews, focus groups, or online research.

➢ **Collect Data**: Gather data from your chosen methods.

➢ **Analyze Data**: Review and interpret the data to identify trends and insights.

➢ **Apply Insights**: Use the findings to refine your services, marketing strategies, and business decisions.

Best Practices:

➢ **Diverse Methods**: Use a combination of qualitative and quantitative research methods for comprehensive insights.

➢ **Regular Updates**: Conduct market research regularly to stay updated with market trends.

Real-Life Examples:

➢ **Case Study**: Jason's market research revealed a demand for executive coaching, leading him to develop a successful new program.

Measurement and Evaluation:

➢ **Data Quality**: Ensure the data collected is accurate and relevant.

➢ **Actionable Insights**: Measure how the insights are applied to improve your business.

➢ **Business Impact**: Track the impact of the research on client acquisition and satisfaction.

Additional Resources:

➢ **Books**: "Market Research in Practice" by Paul Hague.

➢ **Online Courses**: Life Coach Business Masterclass
TransformationAcademy.com/getclients

Action Plan:

➢ **Checklist:**

o Define objectives.

o Choose research methods.

o Collect data.

o Analyze data.

o Apply insights.

➢ **Timeline:**

o Week 1: Define objectives and choose methods.

o Week 2: Collect and analyze data.

o Week 3: Apply insights.

CHAPTER 5:
CLIENT MANAGEMENT AND RETENTION

41. USE CRM TOOLS

Introduction:

> ➢ Customer Relationship Management (CRM) tools help you manage and nurture client relationships effectively.

> ➢ They streamline client communications, track interactions, and improve client retention.

Step-by-Step Guide:

> ➢ **Choose a CRM Tool**: Select a CRM tool that fits your business needs (e.g., HubSpot, Salesforce).

> ➢ **Set Up the CRM**: Import your client data and set up the necessary features.

> ➢ **Organize Client Information**: Organize client data into categories and segments.

> ➢ **Automate Processes**: Use automation features to streamline follow-ups, reminders, and communications.

> ➢ **Track Interactions**: Monitor client interactions and track progress.

> ➤ **Analyze Data**: Use CRM analytics to gain insights into client behavior and preferences.

Best Practices:

> ➤ **Regular Updates**: Keep your CRM data up-to-date for accurate tracking.
> ➤ **Personalization**: Use client data to personalize communications and services.

Real-Life Examples:

> ➤ **Case Study**: Laura's use of a CRM tool improved her client retention rates and streamlined her follow-up process.

Measurement and Evaluation:

> ➤ **Client Engagement**: Track the frequency and quality of client interactions.
> ➤ **Retention Rates**: Measure client retention and repeat business.
> ➤ **Efficiency Gains**: Evaluate the time saved through automation.

Additional Resources:

> ➤ **Books**: "CRM at the Speed of Light" by Paul Greenberg.

Action Plan:

> ➤ **Checklist:**
>   o Choose a CRM tool.
>   o Set up and organize data.
>   o Automate processes.
>   o Track interactions.
>   o Analyze data.

> ➤ **Timeline:**
>   - o Week 1: Choose and set up CRM.
>   - o Week 2: Organize and automate.
>   - o Ongoing: Track and analyze.

42. HOST CLIENT APPRECIATION EVENTS

Introduction:

- ➤ Hosting client appreciation events shows your clients that you value their business and strengthens client relationships.
- ➤ It provides an opportunity to network, receive feedback, and encourage referrals.

Step-by-Step Guide:

- ➤ **Choose a Theme**: Decide on the type of event (e.g., dinner, workshop, party).
- ➤ **Set a Date and Venue**: Choose a convenient date and a suitable venue.
- ➤ **Invite Clients**: Send personalized invitations to your clients.
- ➤ **Plan Activities**: Organize activities, presentations, or giveaways to make the event engaging.
- ➤ **Gather Feedback**: Collect feedback during and after the event to understand client satisfaction.
- ➤ **Follow Up**: Send thank-you notes and share highlights from the event.

Best Practices:

- ➤ **Personal Touch**: Personalize invitations and interactions to make clients feel special.

> **Engaging Activities**: Include activities that encourage networking and interaction.

Real-Life Examples:

> **Case Study**: Amy's annual client appreciation dinner led to increased client loyalty and several new referrals.

Measurement and Evaluation:

> **Attendance Numbers**: Track the number of clients who attend.

> **Client Feedback**: Measure client satisfaction and gather insights for improvement.

> **Referral Rates**: Track the number of referrals received after the event.

Additional Resources:

> **Books**: "The Art of Client Appreciation" by Nancy Friedman.

Action Plan:

> **Checklist:**
>> o Choose theme and set date.
>> o Invite clients.
>> o Plan activities.
>> o Gather feedback.
>> o Follow up.

> **Timeline:**
>> o Week 1: Plan event details.
>> o Week 2: Send invitations.
>> o Week 3: Host event and gather feedback.
>> o Week 4: Follow up.

43. OFFER VIP PACKAGES

Introduction:

➤ VIP packages provide exclusive services and benefits to your top clients, enhancing their experience and loyalty.

➤ They create a sense of exclusivity and can increase client retention and revenue.

Step-by-Step Guide:

➤ **Define VIP Benefits**: Decide on the exclusive services and benefits you will offer (e.g., priority access, additional sessions).

➤ **Set Pricing**: Determine the pricing for your VIP packages.

➤ **Promote VIP Packages**: Advertise the VIP packages to your existing clients and prospects.

➤ **Provide Exceptional Service**: Ensure VIP clients receive top-notch service and attention.

➤ **Gather Feedback**: Collect feedback from VIP clients to improve the packages.

➤ **Adjust and Enhance**: Continuously enhance the VIP packages based on feedback and market trends.

Best Practices:

➤ **Exclusive Benefits**: Offer unique and valuable benefits that justify the premium price.

➤ **Personalized Service**: Provide personalized attention and services to VIP clients.

Real-Life Examples:

➢ **Case Study**: Brian's VIP coaching packages increased his revenue and client satisfaction, with many clients renewing their packages.

Measurement and Evaluation:

➢ **Package Sales**: Track the number of VIP packages sold.
➢ **Client Satisfaction**: Measure satisfaction levels through feedback and surveys.
➢ **Retention Rates**: Track the retention rates of VIP clients.

Additional Resources:

➢ **Books**: "Creating Customer Loyalty Programs" by Fred Reichheld.

Action Plan:

➢ **Checklist:**
   o   Define VIP benefits.
   o   Set pricing.
   o   Promote packages.
   o   Provide service.
   o   Gather feedback.
   o   Adjust and enhance.
➢ **Timeline:**
   o   Week 1: Define benefits and pricing.
   o   Week 2: Promote packages.
   o   Ongoing: Provide service and gather feedback.

44. CREATE INTERACTIVE CONTENT

Introduction:

➢ Interactive content engages your audience and provides a more personalized experience, increasing interest and retention.

➢ It includes quizzes, polls, assessments, and interactive videos.

Step-by-Step Guide:

➢ **Choose Content Type**: Decide on the type of interactive content (e.g., quiz, poll, interactive video).

➢ **Develop Content**: Create the content using tools like Typeform, SurveyMonkey, or interactive video platforms.

➢ **Promote the Content**: Share the interactive content on your website, social media, and email marketing.

➢ **Engage with Participants**: Interact with participants and provide feedback based on their responses.

➢ **Analyze Results**: Review the data and insights gathered from the interactive content.

➢ **Follow Up**: Reach out to participants with additional resources or offers based on their interactions.

Best Practices:

➢ **Engaging Design**: Ensure the content is visually appealing and easy to interact with.

➢ **Value-Driven**: Provide valuable insights or personalized feedback to participants.

Real-Life Examples:

➢ **Case Study**: Jessica's interactive career assessment tool generated leads and provided valuable insights for her coaching services.

Measurement and Evaluation:

- ➤ **Engagement Metrics**: Track participation rates and completion rates.
- ➤ **User Feedback**: Collect feedback from participants on their experience.
- ➤ **Lead Generation**: Measure the number of leads generated from the interactive content.

Additional Resources:

- ➤ **Books**: "Interactive Content Marketing" by Scott Abel.

Action Plan:

- ➤ **Checklist:**
  - o Choose content type.
  - o Develop content.
  - o Promote content.
  - o Engage with participants.
  - o Analyze results.
  - o Follow up.
- ➤ **Timeline:**
  - o Week 1: Choose type and develop content.
  - o Week 2: Promote and engage.
  - o Week 3: Analyze and follow up.

45. IMPLEMENT A FOLLOW-UP SYSTEM

Introduction:

- ➤ A follow-up system ensures that you stay in touch with leads and clients, nurturing relationships and encouraging conversions.
- ➤ It helps manage and automate communications for efficiency.

Step-by-Step Guide:

➢ **Choose a Follow-Up Tool**: Select a CRM or email marketing tool to manage follow-ups.

➢ **Create Follow-Up Sequences**: Develop sequences of emails or messages for different stages of the client journey.

➢ **Automate Follow-Ups**: Use automation features to schedule and send follow-up messages.

➢ **Personalize Communication**: Tailor follow-up messages to address the specific needs and interests of each lead.

➢ **Track and Adjust**: Monitor the performance of your follow-up system and make adjustments as needed.

Best Practices:

➢ **Timely Follow-Ups**: Follow up promptly after initial contact or engagement.

➢ **Consistent Communication**: Maintain regular communication without overwhelming the lead or client.

Real-Life Examples:

➢ **Case Study**: Ben's automated follow-up system increased his client conversion rate by 35%.

Measurement and Evaluation:

➢ **Response Rate**: Track the percentage of leads who respond to follow-ups.

➢ **Conversion Rate**: Measure the percentage of leads who become clients.

➢ **Engagement Metrics**: Monitor open and click-through rates of follow-up emails.

Additional Resources:

➢ **Books**: "Follow Up and Close the Sale" by Jeff Shore.

Action Plan:

➢ **Checklist:**

  o Choose a follow-up tool.

  o Create follow-up sequences.

  o Automate follow-ups.

  o Personalize communication.

  o Track and adjust.

➢ **Timeline:**

  o Week 1: Choose tool and create sequences.

  o Week 2: Automate and personalize.

  o Ongoing: Track and adjust.

46. ATTEND TRADE SHOWS

Introduction:

➢ Trade shows provide opportunities to network, showcase your services, and attract potential clients.

➢ They allow you to engage with a targeted audience interested in your niche.

Step-by-Step Guide:

➢ **Research Trade Shows**: Identify relevant trade shows in your industry.

➢ **Register and Prepare**: Sign up for the trade show and prepare your materials (e.g., business cards, brochures).

➢ **Create an Attractive Booth**: Design a visually appealing booth that draws attention.

> ➤ **Engage Attendees**: Interact with attendees, demonstrate your services, and collect contact information.
> ➤ **Follow Up**: Contact the leads you collected after the trade show with personalized messages.
> ➤ **Evaluate Success**: Assess the outcomes of the trade show, including new leads and potential clients.

Best Practices:

> ➤ **Interactive Booth**: Include interactive elements like demos or presentations to engage attendees.
> ➤ **Professional Appearance**: Ensure your booth and materials are professional and reflective of your brand.

Real-Life Examples:

> ➤ **Case Study**: Karen's participation in a health and wellness trade show resulted in numerous new client sign-ups and collaborations.

Measurement and Evaluation:

> ➤ **Leads Generated**: Track the number of leads collected.
> ➤ **Engagement Metrics**: Measure interactions and interest at the booth.
> ➤ **Client Conversion**: Track the number of leads who become clients.

Additional Resources:

> ➤ **Books**: "Exhibiting at Trade Shows" by Steve Miller

Action Plan:

> ➤ **Checklist:**

- o Research trade shows.
- o Register and prepare.
- o Create an attractive booth.
- o Engage attendees.
- o Follow up.
- o Evaluate success.
- ➤ **Timeline:**
  - o Week 1: Research and register.
  - o Week 2: Prepare materials and booth.
  - o Week 3: Attend and engage.
  - o Week 4: Follow up and evaluate.

47. BUILD A COMMUNITY

Introduction:

- ➤ Building a community around your coaching services fosters engagement, loyalty, and referrals.
- ➤ It creates a supportive environment where clients and prospects can interact and learn from each other.

Step-by-Step Guide:

- ➤ **Choose a Platform**: Decide on a platform for your community (e.g., Facebook Group, LinkedIn Group, forum on your website).
- ➤ **Set Guidelines**: Establish clear rules and guidelines for community interactions.
- ➤ **Promote the Community**: Invite clients and prospects to join through your website, social media, and email marketing.
- ➤ **Engage Regularly**: Post valuable content, moderate discussions, and encourage participation.

- ➤ **Host Events**: Organize virtual events, webinars, and Q&A sessions to keep the community active.
- ➤ **Gather Feedback**: Collect feedback from members to improve the community experience.

Best Practices:

- ➤ **Consistent Engagement**: Regularly post and interact with members to keep the community active.
- ➤ **Value-Driven Content**: Provide valuable resources and support to help members achieve their goals.

Real-Life Examples:

- ➤ **Case Study**: Lisa's LinkedIn group for career development attracted thousands of members, many of whom became paying clients.

Measurement and Evaluation:

- ➤ **Membership Growth**: Track the number of new members joining the community.
- ➤ **Engagement Metrics**: Measure participation, posts, and interactions.
- ➤ **Client Conversion**: Track the number of community members who become clients.

Additional Resources:

- ➤ **Books**: "Buzzing Communities" by Richard Millington

Action Plan:

- ➤ **Checklist:**
  - o Choose platform.
  - o Set guidelines.
  - o Promote the community.

- o Engage regularly.
- o Host events.
- o Gather feedback.
- ➤ **Timeline:**
  - o Week 1: Choose platform and set guidelines.
  - o Week 2: Promote and invite members.
  - o Ongoing: Engage, host events, and gather feedback

48. WRITE FOR INDUSTRY PUBLICATIONS

Introduction:

- ➤ Writing for industry publications establishes you as an authority in your field and reaches a wider audience.
- ➤ It can attract potential clients who read your articles and seek your expertise.

Step-by-Step Guide:

- ➤ **Identify Publications**: Find industry magazines, journals, blogs, and websites that accept guest contributions.
- ➤ **Research Submission Guidelines**: Review the submission guidelines for each publication.
- ➤ **Choose Topics**: Select relevant and valuable topics that showcase your expertise.
- ➤ **Write and Edit Articles**: Write high-quality articles and have them professionally edited.
- ➤ **Submit Articles**: Submit your articles according to the guidelines.
- ➤ **Promote Your Work**: Share published articles on your website, social media, and with your network.

> ➤ **Engage with Readers**: Respond to comments and questions from readers.

Best Practices:

> ➤ **Quality Content**: Ensure your articles provide valuable insights and are well-written.
> ➤ **Consistency**: Regularly contribute to maintain visibility and credibility.

Real-Life Examples:

> ➤ **Case Study**: Tom's articles in a popular business magazine attracted several new clients who appreciated his insights and expertise.

Measurement and Evaluation:

> ➤ **Publication Reach**: Track the reach and readership of your articles.
> ➤ **Engagement Metrics**: Measure comments, shares, and interactions with your articles.
> ➤ **Client Conversion**: Track the number of readers who become clients.

Additional Resources:

> ➤ **Books**: "Everybody Writes" by Ann Handley.

Action Plan:

> ➤ **Checklist:**
>   o Identify publications.
>   o Research guidelines.
>   o Choose topics.
>   o Write and edit articles.
>   o Submit articles.

- o Promote your work.
- o Engage with readers.
- ➢ **Timeline:**
  - o Week 1: Identify and research publications.
  - o Week 2: Choose topics and write articles.
  - o Week 3: Submit and promote.
  - o Ongoing: Engage with readers.

49. CONDUCT FREE ASSESSMENTS

Introduction:

- ➢ Offering free assessments gives potential clients a taste of your coaching services and demonstrates your value.
- ➢ It helps identify their needs and positions you as the solution.

Step-by-Step Guide:

- ➢ **Define the Assessment**: Decide on the type of assessment you will offer (e.g., health assessment, business audit).
- ➢ **Create Assessment Tools**: Develop tools and resources for conducting the assessment (e.g., questionnaires, checklists).
- ➢ **Promote the Offer**: Advertise the free assessment through your website, social media, and email marketing.
- ➢ **Schedule Assessments**: Use a scheduling tool to manage bookings.
- ➢ **Conduct the Assessment**: Provide valuable insights and recommendations during the assessment.
- ➢ **Follow Up**: Send a thank-you email and offer additional coaching services based on the assessment results.

Best Practices:

- ➢ **Value-Driven**: Ensure the assessment provides valuable insights and actionable recommendations.
- ➢ **Personalized Approach**: Tailor the assessment to the individual's specific needs.

Real-Life Examples:

- ➢ **Case Study**: David's free business audit attracted several new clients who were impressed with his insights and recommendations.

Measurement and Evaluation:

- ➢ **Number of Assessments**: Track the number of assessments conducted.
- ➢ **Client Feedback**: Collect feedback from participants on their experience.
- ➢ **Conversion Rate**: Track the percentage of assessments that lead to client sign-ups.

Additional Resources:

- ➢ **Books**: "Consultative Selling" by Mack Hanan.

Action Plan:

- ➢ **Checklist:**
  - ○ Define the assessment.
  - ○ Create assessment tools.
  - ○ Promote the offer.
  - ○ Schedule assessments.
  - ○ Conduct assessments.
  - ○ Follow up.

> ➤ **Timeline:**
>   - ○ Week 1: Define and create tools.
>   - ○ Week 2: Promote and schedule.
>   - ○ Ongoing: Conduct and follow up.

50. ENGAGE IN PUBLIC SPEAKING

Introduction:

> ➤ Public speaking establishes you as an expert and allows you to reach a large audience.
> ➤ It provides opportunities to showcase your knowledge and attract potential clients.

Step-by-Step Guide:

> ➤ **Identify Speaking Opportunities**: Look for conferences, seminars, workshops, and webinars where you can speak.
> ➤ **Create a Compelling Presentation**: Develop a presentation that provides valuable insights and engages the audience.
> ➤ **Pitch Your Speaking Services**: Contact event organizers with your speaking proposal.
> ➤ **Prepare Thoroughly**: Practice your presentation to ensure it flows well and fits the allotted time.
> ➤ **Engage the Audience**: Use interactive elements and encourage audience participation.
> ➤ **Follow Up**: Network with attendees after the event and follow up with leads.

Best Practices:

> ➤ **Engaging Content**: Ensure your presentation is informative, engaging, and relevant to the audience.

➤ **Confidence**: Deliver your presentation with confidence and enthusiasm.

Real-Life Examples:

➤ **Case Study**: Mark's keynote speech at a business conference led to multiple new client sign-ups and increased visibility.

Measurement and Evaluation:

➤ **Audience Size**: Track the number of attendees.
➤ **Engagement Metrics**: Measure audience engagement through questions, feedback, and interactions.
➤ **Client Conversion**: Track the number of leads who become clients.

Additional Resources:

➤ **Books**: "Talk Like TED" by Carmine Gallo.
➤ **Online Courses**: Life Coach Business Masterclass TransformationAcademy.com/getclients

Action Plan:

➤ **Checklist:**
  o Identify opportunities.
  o Create presentation.
  o Pitch services.
  o Prepare thoroughly.
  o Engage the audience.
  o Follow up.
➤ **Timeline:**
  o Week 1: Identify opportunities and create presentation.
  o Week 2: Pitch and prepare.
  o Week 3: Present and follow up.

CONGRATULATIONS!

Congratulations! You've made it through "50 Proven Ways to Market Your Life Coaching Business." You've now got a toolkit brimming with strategies to attract clients, build your brand, and grow your coaching practice. As you wrap up this mini book, let's take a moment to reflect on what you've learned and how to take these insights forward.

YOUR MARKETING MASTERY

By now, you should have a good understanding of the diverse marketing techniques available to you. From harnessing the power of social media and creating compelling content to engaging in public speaking and networking, you've got a plethora of options to explore. Remember, the key to success lies in choosing the right mix of strategies that align with your strengths, resonate with your audience, and fit your business goals.

THE JOURNEY AHEAD

Marketing is not a one-and-done deal; it's a journey. As you step out to implement these strategies, keep these essential points in mind:

➢ **Stay Consistent**: Consistency is your best friend. Regular efforts, no matter how small, add up over time. Whether it's posting on social media, sending newsletters, or attending events, stick with it.

1. **Be Adaptable**: Flexibility is crucial. Not every strategy will hit the mark immediately. Don't be afraid to pivot, tweak, and refine your approach. Learn from what works and what doesn't, and keep evolving.

2. **Engage and Connect**: At the heart of every successful marketing strategy is genuine engagement. Whether online or offline, focus on building real connections. Your authenticity and passion will shine through and attract clients who resonate with your message.

3. **Measure and Improve**: Use the metrics and evaluation tips provided with each strategy to track your progress. Analyzing your efforts helps you understand what's working and where there's room for improvement.

4. **Keep Learning**: The marketing landscape is always changing. Stay curious and keep learning. Attend workshops, read new books, follow industry leaders, and never stop expanding your knowledge.

A FINAL WORD OF ENCOURAGEMENT

As you embark on this exciting journey of marketing your coaching business, remember to enjoy the process. Yes, there will be challenges and setbacks, but there will also be victories and moments of joy. Embrace them all with a positive mindset and a dash of humor.

Think of marketing as an ongoing experiment. Some ideas will take off like a rocket, while others might need more nurturing or a different approach. Stay patient, stay persistent, and most importantly, stay true to yourself and the unique value you bring as a coach.

THANK YOU AND BEST WISHES

Thank you for choosing this mini book as your marketing guide. Your dedication to growing your coaching business and serving your clients is truly inspiring. As you implement these strategies, we hope you find success, fulfillment, and a thriving community of clients who benefit from your expertise.

Now, go out there and make your mark! The world needs your coaching, and with these proven marketing strategies, you're well-equipped to reach those who need your guidance. Here's to your continued growth and success!

Happy marketing, and keep shining bright!

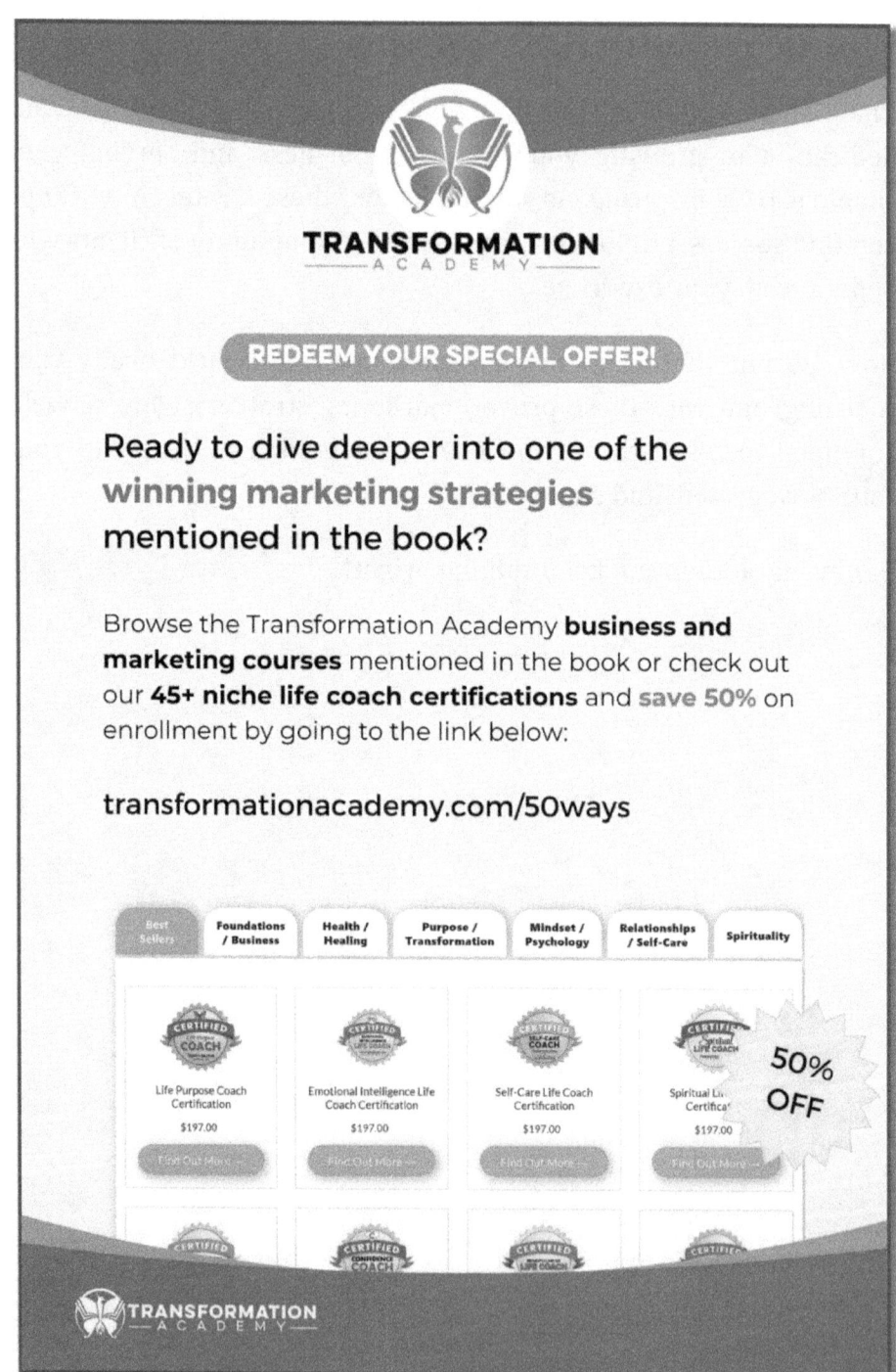

www.ingramcontent.com/pod-product-compliance
Lightning Source LLC
Chambersburg PA
CBHW070107230526
45472CB00004B/1160